CAUSES AND CONSEQUENCES

OF THE

ARAB-ISRAELI
CONFLICT

CAUSES AND CONSEQUENCES

OF THE

ARAB-ISRAELI
CONFLICT

STEWART ROSS

RSVP
RAINTREE
STECK-VAUGHN
PUBLISHERS
The Steck-Vaughn Company

Austin, Texas

Published by Raintree Steck-Vaughn Publishers,
an imprint of Steck-Vaughn Company

Developed by the Creative Publishing Company
Editor: Sabrina Crewe
Designed by Ian Winton

Raintree Steck-Vaughn Publishers staff
Project Manager: Joyce Spicer
Editor: Shirley Shalit
Electronic Production: Scott Melcer
Consultant: Christopher S. Taylor, Drew University

Cover photo (large): Palestinians throw rocks during an anti-Israeli demonstration.
Cover photo (small): An Israeli soldier joins other Jews in prayer at the Western Wall in Jerusalem, 1995.

Library of Congress Cataloging-in-Publication Data

Ross, Stewart.
    Arab-Israeli conflict / Stewart Ross.
       p.   cm. – (Causes and consequences)
    Includes bibliographical references and index.
    ISBN 0-8172-4051-9
    1. Israel-Arab conflicts — Juvenile literature.   2. Jewish-Arab
relations — 1949- — Juvenile literature. I. Title. II. Series.
DS119.7.R6725   1995
956.9404–dc20   95-17097
                                                   CIP   AC

Printed in Hong Kong
Bound in the United States
1 2 3 4 5 6 7 8 9 0 LB 99 98 97 96 95

CONTENTS

THE WORLD'S ANGRY REGION

The ongoing conflict — Israeli soldiers grapple with a Palestinian woman as she tries to prevent the arrest of a young man in Gaza, January 1, 1994.

Since the end of World War II in 1945, scarcely a day has passed when the Middle East has not been in the news. For decades the reporting was largely of tragedy — war, terrorism, hostages, and destruction. Recent announcements have struck a more optimistic note, talking of troop withdrawals and peace treaties. And in all these reports, whether they bear good news or bad, the same two words crop up time and again: Arab and Israeli.

The Arabs are a people united by a common language, history, and culture. They do not all share the same faith. Although most are Muslims, several million, notably in Egypt and Lebanon, are Christian. Arabs make up the bulk of the population in Morocco, Algeria, Tunisia, and Libya, and the majority of the

countries of the Middle East. During the nineteenth century most Arabs outside the remote desert regions of Arabia lived under the imperial rule of the Ottoman Empire, France, or Britain. These empires crumbled in the twentieth century and, in their place, independent Arab states were established. However, during this process, especially between the two world wars, the Arab world became infuriated by efforts to create a new Jewish state in Palestine, at that time an area with a majority Arab population.

Hope for the future as U.S. President Bill Clinton plays host to Israeli prime minister Yitzhak Rabin (left) and PLO chairman Yasir Arafat (right) for the Israeli-PLO peace accord, September 1993.

7

We accept no kind of co-existence with Israel. The rights of the Palestinians should be given back to them. What happened in 1948 was an aggression against the people of Palestine. Israel expelled the Palestinians from their country and stole their property.

President Gamal Abdul Nasser of Egypt, May 28, 1967

The new state was Israel. Although conflict between the Arabs and the Jews began much earlier, the modern Arab-Israeli military conflict started on the day of Israel's foundation, May 14, 1948.

Israel was established as a homeland for the Jewish people. Like the Arabs, the Jews were without their own nation. They too were bound together by language, culture, history, and religion. In ancient times they inhabited the biblical land of Israel in Palestine. Having fallen under Roman rule, in A.D. 67 they revolted against their conquerors. It took six years for the Romans to put down the revolt and expel the Jewish people from Israel. This expulsion is known as the Diaspora.

For centuries the Jews lived in widespread communities in different parts of the world, although some never left Palestine. Jewish communities grew up in most Middle Eastern and European lands and also in the Americas and the Far East. The Jews were an easily distinguished minority. Since the time of Christ, they have been especially subjected to harsh persecution in some Christian countries and were often not allowed to mix freely with other peoples. Some Christians blamed the Jews for the death of Jesus. Jews were envied and criticized when they achieved commercial success. Frequently non-Jewish communities made them scapegoats for ills beyond their control, such as famine, plague, and economic recession. During the Nazi occupation of most of Europe, Jews suffered unspeakable atrocities and even death by the millions.

The persecuted people of Europe — Jews being led away to Nazi extermination camps following the collapse of the rising in the Warsaw ghetto, 1943.

Since the Diaspora, Jews dreamed that one day they would return to their homeland in Palestine. Until the late nineteenth century the notion of a return to the land of Israel was primarily religious in its intent. From the late nineteenth century onward this idea was transformed into a doctrine of political nationalism, and it began to attract support among both religious and non-religious Jews.

This ambition of creating a modern nation-state was not unique to the Jews. In many parts of the world in the nineteenth century, people of the same culture and background — including Arabs — were aspiring to their own nation-states. The situation in the Middle East was further complicated when Britain, eager for support against Turkey in World War I, promised both Arab independence from Turkish rule, which would have enabled Arabs and Palestinians to establish their own nation-states, and a Palestinian homeland to the Jews. Eventually, with the backing of some, but not all, of the victors of World War II, the state of Israel was established.

The consequences of this final action rumble on to this day: The Middle East was more destabilized than usual, making it one of the world's most troubled regions. Arabs were both divided and united. A large number of Palestinian Arabs became second-class citizens in an alien state. Palestinians decided to form their own resistance organization (the Palestine Liberation Organization, or PLO), dedicated to opposing the Israelis by whatever means they could, including terrorism and hostage taking. Citizens of the new state were suspicious, intolerant, and defensive. Four major wars and countless bloody skirmishes ensued, which racked and distorted the economies of Israel and its neighbors. The conflict was linked with an oil embargo that rocked the world economy. The United States came to the brink of war with the Soviet Union. Politicians were brought down, tortured, and assassinated.

Finally, however, years of conflict have led to a quest for peace. The first breakthrough came in 1977 on the initiative of President Anwar Sadat of Egypt. Gradually other Arab states joined the process and by 1994, of the major Arab states, only Syria still declared itself at war with Israel. Whether or not this signals the final end of the Arab-Israeli conflict only time will tell. But for the moment no picture of the modern world is complete without an understanding of the causes and consequences of this most bitter and crippling of conflicts.

President Carter once said that the United States is committed without reservation to seeing the peace process through until all parties to the Arab-Israeli conflict are at peace. We value such a promise from a leader who raised the banners of morality as a substitute for power politics and opportunism.

President Anwar Sadat of Egypt, March 26, 1979

9

TWO PEOPLES, ONE LAND

THE NATION-STATE

The Turkish Ottoman Empire at the outbreak of World War I in 1914. The breakup of the empire after the war created the opportunity for a Jewish homeland in Palestine.

Over the last hundred years politicians of every continent have divided the surface of the world into countries, or nation-states. There are almost two hundred separate nation-states, each with its own flag, government, and national identity. There are nations whose people are divided through intolerance of each other's race, culture, religion, or political beliefs. These nations run the risk of splitting into a number of smaller states. This happened to the Soviet Union, Yugoslavia, and Czechoslovakia in the 1990s.

The nation-state is a relatively new concept. In the Middle Ages, for example, the people of Europe had a sense of belonging to Christendom as much as to a

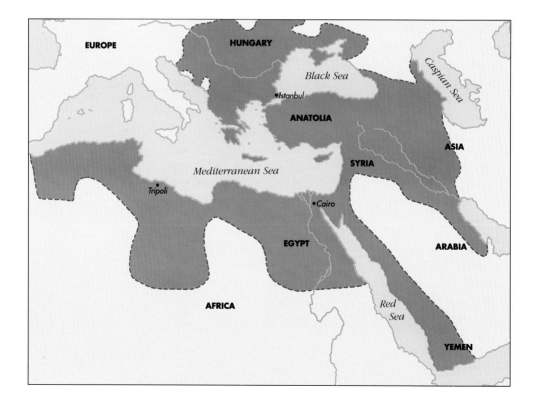

particular kingdom. Similarly, the Arab people thought of themselves as members of the Muslim world. For Africans the tribe was the focus of loyalty, not a country.

Although there had been countries with a strong sense of national unity since medieval times, the true age of the nation-state began in the nineteenth century. By 1880 the small states and cities of Germany and Italy had joined together to form single nations. Farther east, the subject peoples of the Ottoman Empire began to break away from Turkish rule and form nations of their own. Western imperialist powers gathered colonies around the world. When these colonies acquired independence in the twentieth century, they too became new nation-states. The two great international organizations of the twentieth century, the League of Nations and the United Nations, were based on membership of nation-states. Pride in one's nation, or nationalism, became a major political force.

The search for nationhood affected all peoples. Those without a nation of their own were seen as "stateless," second-class citizens. Consequently, they felt a powerful need to belong, to create a nation-state of their own. No two peoples have felt this need more strongly than the Jews and the Palestinians.

The reawakening of the Arab nation, and the mounting efforts of the Jews to rebuild the ancient monarchy of Israel on a massive scale — these two movements are bound to fight continually, until one defeats the other.

N. Azouri, The Awakening of the Arab Nation Against the Asian Turk, 1905

PALESTINE

Palestine is the name that the Romans gave to the area of land between the Jordan River and the Mediterranean after they had exiled most of the Jews from the region. In biblical times the area lay at the heart of the Jewish kingdom of King Solomon, commonly known as Israel. Palestine is sometimes termed the Holy Land because certain places, notably the city of Jerusalem, played a special part in the Jewish, Muslim, and Christian religions. After World War I this area of land was freed from centuries of Turkish rule, made a mandate by the League of Nations, and named Palestine.

Jews and Arabs are both Semitic peoples, which means they speak closely related Semitic languages. There have always been Jews and Arabs living in the Palestine region. In A.D. 637 the area was conquered by the Muslim Arabs, who treated their Jewish neighbors relatively well. The Christian crusaders, who held various parts of Palestine from 1099 until 1291, by com-

11

parison, persecuted the Jews mercilessly. The region was then governed by Turkish Muslims, first the Mamluks (1291–1516), and then the Ottomans (1517–1917). The Turks tolerated the Jewish religion, and even welcomed Jewish refugees from Christian persecution in Europe. Some estimates suggest that by 1800 the majority of the population of Jerusalem were Jews. Although there were sporadic incidents of racial and religious unrest, Jews and Arabs lived for centuries in relative harmony under their Turkish masters.

JEWISH AND ARAB NATIONALISM

Theodore Herzl (1860–1904), the Austrian Jew who called the first Zionist Congress at Basel in 1897, launching the movement for an independent Jewish homeland.

In the later nineteenth century two movements arose that shattered the harmony of Palestine and laid the foundations for the Arab-Israeli conflict. These movements were Jewish nationalism (also known as Zionism after *Zion*, the ancient Jewish name for Jerusalem) and Arab nationalism. In other words, both the Arabs and the Jews wanted self-rule in their own nation-state.

The modern movement for a Jewish homeland grew out of a series of violent attacks, known as pogroms, on the Russian Jews in the early 1880s. In 1882 a group of Jewish exiles met in Constantinople. Calling themselves "Lovers of Zion," they issued a manifesto in which they called for "a home in our country. It was given to us by the mercy of God; it is ours as registered in the archives of history."

These people believed that God had given Palestine to the Jews. The problem was that by the 1880s most people who lived in Palestine were not Jewish but Arab. This was a sure recipe for future disaster.

Zionism became a political movement under the leadership of an Austrian Jew named Theodore Herzl (1860–1904), who organized Zionist conferences and set out his plans in a

Jewish immigrants to Palestine building the new town of Tel Aviv, founded in 1909. Arabs watched the construction of the first entirely Jewish town with dismay.

pamphlet entitled *The Jewish State.* A World Zionist Organization was formed in 1897 and the number of Jews emigrating to Palestine increased quite sharply. Some sources (probably favoring Jewish claims to Israel) say that between 1880 and 1914 over 60,000 Jews arrived, mostly from Eastern Europe. The population of Palestine by 1914 has been estimated at half a million Arabs and between 50,000 and 90,000 Jews.

In 1909 an entirely Jewish town, Tel Aviv, was founded alongside the Port of Jaffa. This marked a worrying trend — the separation of Jew from Arab. The immigrants bought land, often from Arabs, and established their own communities. Only in the large cities did the two peoples live side by side.

While a distinct Palestinian nationalism did not emerge as a major force until after World War II, a more general movement, Arab nationalism, began to make itself felt in the first years of the twentieth century. It found a voice in the journalist Negib Azouri, who edited a magazine called *Arab Independence* which supported a League of the Arab Fatherland. Azouri wanted the Arab peoples released from Turkish rule and free to govern themselves in an Arab empire. Although he preached religious toleration, the concept of an Arab Fatherland did not accord well with what was happening in Palestine.

In 1886 the first attack by Arabs on Jewish settlements occurred. Five years later a group of Palestinian Arabs petitioned the Turkish government in Constantinople to halt Jewish immigration into Palestine. In 1914 six anti-Zionist societies were set up, four in Palestine and one each in Beirut and Constantinople.

The Jewish question is . . . a national question. We are a people — one people. Wherever we have lived, we have honestly tried to mix in socially with other people, while at the same time keeping our religion. But we have not been allowed to do this . . . .

The answer, therefore, is simple . . . . Give us control over part of the globe big enough to meet the Jews' rightful needs; the rest we shall manage for ourselves.

Theodore Herzl, The Jewish State, *1896*

THE WAR YEARS

BRITAIN AND THE MIDDLE EAST

Just when tension between the Arabs and Jews in Palestine was building, the situation was suddenly complicated further by the outbreak of World War I. The Arab world became involved because, on November 5, 1914, Britain declared war on Turkey, an ally of Germany. Neither France nor Russia (Britain's allies) was in a position to commit troops to the Middle East. Britain already had a strong interest in the region, controlling Egypt and key points at the southern end of the Arabian peninsula. This control was essential to safeguard the Suez Canal and the route to India, Britain's most valued colony. The British were also eager to see that the Middle East oil fields did not

During World War I the future of the Ottoman lands was often disputed. The Sykes-Picot Agreement of 1916 was a secret plan to divide captured territory into five territories, but it made no provision for a Jewish homeland. Although a crucial part of Anglo-French negotiations, the Sykes-Picot plan was never used.

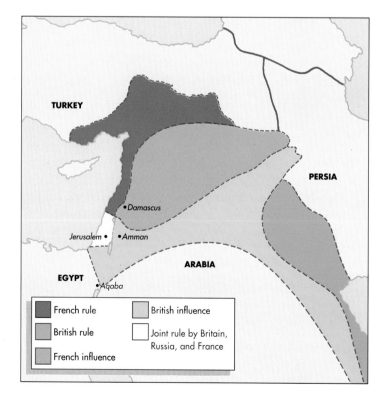

TURKEY

PERSIA

•Damascus

Jerusalem •   •Amman

ARABIA

EGYPT

•Aqaba

French rule

British rule

French influence

British influence

Joint rule by Britain, Russia, and France

fall into hostile hands, and so they undertook to oppose the Turks.

Britain's task was daunting. Ottoman territory in the Middle East stretched from Turkey itself to Aqaba and Mecca in the west and Basra at the head of the Persian Gulf in the east. Moreover, the Turks had held their Arab empire for centuries. They knew it intimately and were experienced at fighting in its arid regions. The sort of setback feared by the British happened in April 1916, when the Turks forced the surrender of an Anglo-Indian force at Kut, in Mesopotamia (now Iraq). The British had already realized that to have any hope of success, they needed an ally. This ally could only be the Arabs.

BRITAIN AND THE ARABS

The British high commissioner in Cairo, Sir Henry McMahon, negotiated with Hussein ibn Ali, the sherif of Mecca, who hoped to be the first leader of an independent Arab state. From the British he sought recognition of his claim and a joint operation against the Turks.

A number of letters passed between the two men, the most important of which was written by McMahon on October 24, 1915. It was not clearly written and began by excluding from any agreement the "portions of Syria lying to the west of the district[s] of Damascus . . . [as they] cannot be said to be purely Arab." It also said that Britain could not be bound by any agreement that might run against French interests. "Subject to the above modifications," it went on, "Great Britain is prepared to recognize and support the independence of the Arabs in all the regions within the limits demanded by the Sherif of Mecca."

By September 1918 Hussein and the British under General Edmund Allenby had defeated the Turks and entered Damascus. The time had come, Hussein demanded, for the British to honor their promise to him. But it was not to be.

The British pointed out the reservations in McMahon's letter. They also referred to other letters between the high commissioner and Hussein, which had failed to agree over who should control the area to the west of the Jordan. The words "Palestine," "Jerusalem," and "Jews" had never been mentioned by either party.

Major General Edmund Allenby (1861–1936), the British commander who was moved from the Western front to the Middle East in 1917. His skillful campaign against the Turks led to the capture of Jerusalem and Damascus.

But if that was bad for Hussein, there was more bad news. During the war Britain had made two other agreements regarding the Middle East. Both contradicted the pledge made to the sherif of Mecca.

BRITAIN AND FRANCE

Shortly after the outbreak of World War I, Great Britain and France started negotiating about what they would do with the Ottoman Empire when the war was over. The two nations assumed, of course, that they would win. A secret plan, known as the Sykes-Picot Agreement, was prepared by Sir Mark Sykes and Charles Georges-Picot and accepted by both governments in 1916.

The Sykes-Picot Agreement divided the Ottoman Arab lands into five categories. Some were to be under direct French or British rule, other parts were designated Arab states, but under British or French "influence." Finally, a region (roughly the area of Palestine) around the holy places was to be under the joint control of Britain, Russia, and France. There was no mention of a separate homeland for the Jews, but neither was there any attempt to honor the understanding entered into with Hussein. A third promise, delivered the year after the Sykes-Picot Agreement, made the situation even more complicated.

BRITAIN AND THE JEWS

1917 was a hard year for Britain. The war seemed to be dragging on forever, at a huge cost in men, materials, and money. In November, Arthur Balfour (1848–1930), the British foreign minister, sent a letter to Lord Lionel Rothschild, a prominent Jewish banker and supporter of Zionism. In the letter Balfour offered his government's support for "the establishment in Palestine of a national home for the Jewish people."

Ever since, people have wondered why the Balfour Declaration was made. It contradicted the Sykes-Picot Agreement and the understanding between Hussein

Arthur James Balfour (center), the British foreign secretary whose famous Balfour Declaration of 1917 promised a national home for the Jews in Palestine and appeared to run contrary to previous British promises to their Arab allies. The figure on the right is Dr. Chaim Weizmann (1874–1952), the Zionist leader credited with a prominent role in securing the Declaration.

and McMahon. Three reasons for Balfour's behavior have been suggested. Firstly, Britain was wooing prominent Jews, whose support was needed at home, in the United States, and in Russia. Secondly, it is thought that Balfour wanted a state friendly to Britain in the eastern Mediterranean, to safeguard the Suez Canal and act as a buffer between French-controlled Syria and British-controlled Egypt. Finally, the Zionist leader Chaim Weizmann got on well with the leading members of the British government, many of whom felt sorry for the Jews and wished to help them.

THE MANDATES

By the time World War I ended, therefore, Britain had made three different and, some may say, contradictory proposals: (1) to help the Arabs set up their own states in the Middle East; (2) to divide the region between Britain and France; and (3) to give the Jews their own "national home" in Palestine. At the 1919 peace talks, it was an Anglo-French plan — though not the Sykes-Picot Agreement — that was finally accepted. The former Ottoman Arab lands were put in the hands of Britain and France, who were to look after them and prepare them for self-government. Britain received Iraq, Transjordan, and Palestine, while France was given Syria and Lebanon. Iraq became independent in 1932, and Lebanon, Syria, and Transjordan, did so in 1946. In taking over Palestine, however, the British had landed themselves with a problem for which they had no solution.

An answer seemed to be to divide Palestine into two states, one Arab and the other Jewish. In 1919 this appeared to have been agreed between Chaim Weizmann and Hussein's son, Faisal, who later became king of Iraq. However other Arab leaders rejected the plan, and in 1929 Faisal himself said that he had come to no such understanding. Sporadic fighting between Jews and Arabs broke out in 1920. The following year the British stated that they had never intended the whole of Palestine to become a Jewish state. But the time for compromise had passed. After the three different proposals of the war years, neither the Jews nor the Arabs trusted their British overlords. A full-blown Arab-Jewish conflict in Palestine was now almost a certainty.

We Arabs, especially the educated among us, look with the deepest sympathy on the Zionist movement. [We are] . . . fully acquainted with the proposals submitted yesterday [March 2, 1919] by the Zionist Organization to the Peace Conference, and we regard them as moderate and proper. We will do our best . . . to help them through: we will wish the Jews a most hearty welcome home.

Letter from Faisal ibn Hussein to the leader of the Jewish delegation at the 1919 Versailles Peace Conference, March 3, 1919 (Faisal later denied authorship)

THE WEAK POLICEMAN

THE BRITISH IN PALESTINE

In theory the League of Nations was responsible for the former German and Turkish colonies taken over as mandates after World War I. In practice they handed over this responsibility to certain of the victorious nations, in effect adding to those nations' already large colonial empires.

In many ways Britain was not the right country to be given responsibility for overseeing Palestine and bringing it to self-government. Britain's primary interest in the region was not fulfilling the wishes of the local people, but safeguarding the Suez Canal and the route to India. Furthermore, by its deeds and actions during the war, Britain had lost the trust of both the Arab and Jewish communities.

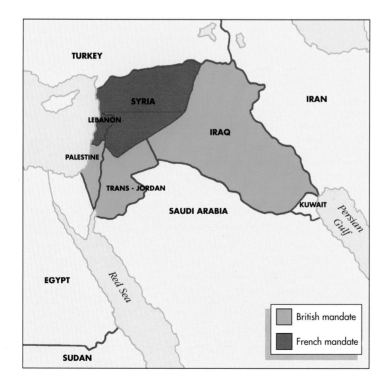

The Middle East mandates after World War I, which gave responsibility for Palestine and some of its neighbors to Britain and France. Egypt was also a British protectorate until 1922.

To deal with the ex-Turkish provinces not considered ready for independence, British colonial secretary Winston Churchill (front row, center) called the Cairo Conference of 1921. Also in attendance are T. E. Lawrence ("Lawrence of Arabia." fourth from the right, second row) and Sir Herbert Samuel, on Churchill's right.

Arab hopes had been raised by McMahon's declaration of support for Arab independence, then dashed by his government's failure to follow this up. The Arabs had been further annoyed by the Balfour Declaration and the apparent support for the Jewish cause among leading British politicians. An example of this support came in 1921 when the British colonial secretary Winston Churchill declared ". . . it is manifestly right that the Jews, who are scattered all over the world, should have a . . . National Home where some of them may be united. Where else could this be but in this land of Palestine, with which for more than three thousand years they have been intimately and profoundly associated? We think it will be good for the world, good for the Jews and good for the British Empire."

The Jews, too, also had reason to mistrust the British. The Balfour Declaration, which directly contradicted the Sykes-Picot Agreement, seemed to them a cynical bid for support at a time when British fortunes were at a low ebb. In the period of the British mandate over Palestine (1920–48) the fears of both Arab and Jew were fueled by Britain's indecisive and wavering attitude. Sometimes, such as when they set limits on Jewish immigration, they appeared to support the Arabs. More often, particularly in their treatment of Arab resistance, it looked as if they were backing the Jews.

Above all, the British seemed to have no policy toward Palestine other than trying to contain the violence. In the light of the Arab-Israeli agreements reached in the 1990s, probably the only solution would have been to have divided Palestine between Arab and Jewish areas as soon as the mandate had been established. Although suggested, this was never done. As a result, Britain was seen as a weak and biased policeman unable to control a beat for which he was not really concerned, and British officials and soldiers became targets for both sides. Britain's inept handling of the problems of the mandate, therefore, was a major cause of the future Arab-Israeli conflict.

IMMIGRATION AND RESISTANCE

One of Britain's first mistakes was to appoint a Jew, Sir Herbert Samuel, as high commissioner of Palestine. He held the post until 1925. His report on leaving his post made quite clear where his sympathies lay. When he arrived in Palestine, he recalled, the Valley of Jezreel "was a desolation." All he saw were "four or five squalid Arab villages." Otherwise there was "not a house, not a tree." In contrast, by 1925, after five years of Jewish settlement and an investment of almost a million Egyptian pounds, "The whole aspect of the valley has been changed . . . . In the spring the fields of vegetables or of cereals cover many miles of land, and what five years ago was little better than a desert is being transformed before our eyes into smiling countryside." The words "squalid" and "smiling," contrasting Arab and Jewish lifestyles, do not suggest an unbiased viewpoint.

Britain's problems began in 1920, when Arabs attacked Jewish settlements and caused four of them to be abandoned. By the end of the year it is believed about 10,000 Jewish immigrants had arrived since the end of World War I. They had established their own defense force, the Haganah, and the General Federation of Jewish Labor, which promoted further immigration and settlement. The Arabs asked the British to establish Palestinian self-rule before the Jews gained an even stronger hold over the land. The British refused, but in September 1920 they limited Jewish immigration to 16,500 a year; the following

So far as the Arabs are concerned . . . I hope they will remember that it is we who have established an independent Arab sovereignty of the Hedjaz [Arabia]. I hope they will remember it is we who desire in Mesopotamia [Iraq] to prepare the way for . . . a self-governing . . . Arab state, and I hope that, remembering all that, they will not grudge that small notch — for it is no more than that geographically, whatever it may be historically — that small notch in what are now Arab territories being given to the people [the Jews] who for all these hundreds of years have been separated from it.

Arthur Balfour, July 12, 1920

*A city at peace —
Jerusalem, 1925.
During the mid-
1920s Arab and
Jew coexisted in
relative harmony.*

year all immigration was temporarily suspended. However it is estimated that the Jewish population of Palestine doubled between 1918 and 1929. In 1929 an official British estimate suggested that if Jews entered Palestine at the rate of 15,000 a year, the Jewish population would equal that of the Arabs by 1956. It is often forgotten that the Jews were not the only immigrants into Palestine — figures indicate 50,000 Arabs also entered the country between 1919 and 1939.

Tension between Arabs and Jews died down at the end of 1921 but flared up again in 1929 with a series of anti-Jewish riots, some marked by extreme cruelty. Once again the British were caught in the middle. The Jerusalem riot of August 23, 1929, left 133 Jews and 116 Arabs dead. Of the latter, 110 had been killed by the British police. While the Arabs accused the British of treating them like "naughty children," the Jews said the mandate government deprived them of the means to defend themselves, "giving the murderers and robbers their chance."

In 1936 the Arabs began a general strike in which they were led by their spiritual leader, the grand mufti of Jerusalem. This was followed by a major anti-Jewish and anti-British uprising. The country descended into chaos as Arabs attacked Jews, the

British, and even fellow Arabs who sympathized with the Jewish cause, and Jews fought back against the Arabs. The British moved 20,000 troops into the region to restore order. One British officer, Orde Wingate, even organized Jewish Special Night Squads to attack Arab villages. It was hardly the sort of move that would bring peace or allay Arab fears. The squads' tactics were often as brutal as anything of which the Arabs had been accused.

By the later 1930s, therefore, the British had failed to control Arab-Jewish hostility, which was approaching new heights of ferocity. Furthermore, in central Europe a series of events was already under way that would change Palestine's internal problem into a war between nations. In 1933 the Nazis came to power in Germany and the last seed of the future Arab-Israeli conflict was sown.

Wingate . . . went up to the four Arab prisoners. He said in Arabic, "You have arms in the village. Where have you hidden them?" The Arabs shook their heads. Wingate reached down and took sand from the ground. He thrust it into the mouth of the first Arab and pushed it down until he puked.

Cited in Walter Oppenheim, The Middle East, Blackwell, 1989

A city in turmoil — Jaffa, 1933. Arabs demonstrating against Jewish immigration into Palestine confront British police. Some forty people, British and Arab, were killed.

PERSECUTION AND PARTITION

THE HOLOCAUST

The Jews had been persecuted throughout the history of Christian Europe. Individuals, families, even whole communities had been beaten up or killed and their property stolen or destroyed. Sometimes a country had expelled all Jews living there. But nothing in Europe's past equaled the sickening horror of Nazi anti-Semitism. Beginning with discrimination in 1933, it grew to vicious persecution and ended with the Holocaust — a cold-blooded attempt to exterminate all Jews from Nazi-held lands. Estimates of the number of Jews killed vary from five to eleven million.

Nazi anti-Semitism raised two emotions in the hearts of the leaders of the Western powers — guilt and sympathy. Both ensured that after the war they swung strongly behind the Palestinian Jews and supported the foundation of the state of Israel. When the awful truth of what had been going on in the slaughter pits and extermination camps of the Third Reich became apparent, Western sympathy for the Jews was immediate and understandable. The West's guilt, however, requires some explanation.

Between 1933 and 1945 the countries in a position to shelter refugees from Nazi persecution put concerns about domestic unemployment above humanitarian assistance. Brazil, Spain, Australia, and South Africa, for example, placed severe limits on Jewish immigration. India, Turkey, and Mexico were virtually closed. Britain and the United States limited by quota systems the numbers of refugees they would accept. In 1941 the United States Congress rejected a proposal to stretch the quota to allow the entry of 20,000 German-Jewish children. Two years later the British government rejected an appeal by the Archbishop of Canterbury to abolish its quota system. In the same year the United States State Department turned down a Swedish plan to rescue another 20,000 Jewish children from Germany.

The saddest example of the manner in which

(I) That Jew shall not dominate Arab and Arab shall not dominate Jew in Palestine. (II) That Palestine shall be neither a Jewish nor an Arab state. (III) That the form of government ultimately to be established, shall under international guarantees, fully protect and preserve the interests in the Holy Land of Christendom and of the Moslem and Jewish faiths.

Recommendations of the Anglo-American Committee of Enquiry into the condition of the Jewish people, May 1, 1945

Jewish refugees were shunned by officialdom was the story of the voyage of the liner *St. Louis.* Carrying 930 Jewish refugees, on May 13, 1939, the ship left Germany bound for the United States. Most of the passengers had permission to enter the United States within three years, and all held Cuban landing certificates. However, the Cubans permitted only twenty-two to come ashore. The United States accepted not one. Its example was followed by several South American countries. In June the ship returned to Europe, where Britain, Holland, and Belgium agreed to take the refugees. Those who ended up in mainland Europe came under Nazi rule within the year. Many were exterminated. The 287 who had landed in Britain were imprisoned as "enemy aliens" on the outbreak of war. In the light of tales such as this, it is hardly surprising that the appeal for a Jewish homeland was favorably received in 1945. The Arab cause was not helped by the fact that the grand mufti of Jerusalem had attempted to gain Hitler's support.

Jewish families prepare to flee the Baltic port of Memel in March 1939, as German troops move in and the Nazi swastika is raised over Jewish homes.

THE LAST DAYS OF PALESTINE

Nazi persecution increased the number of Jewish refugees seeking entry into Palestine. This in turn fueled Arab-Jewish tension and made Britain's task of governing the Palestinian mandate even more difficult.

An anti-Semitic poster from a Nazi exhibition of 1937, entitled "The Eternal Jew." The persecution of Jews aroused sympathy and guilt around the world, leading many countries to support the foundation of Israel.

The fighting of 1936 continued into 1938 and 1939. As well as employing peacekeeping forces, Britain also tried to stop the fighting by diplomatic means. A Royal Commission was set up in 1936 to report on how the government of the mandate was progressing. The result was the Peel Commission Report of 1937. It recommended that Palestine be divided into three parts: a small Jewish state in the north, a large Arab state in the south, and a small tongue of land stretching from the coast to the holy places remaining under British control. The Jews reluctantly accepted the Peel Commision Report proposal. The Arabs rejected it outright. They would not surrender a single piece of land that was, they claimed, inherently theirs. The terrorism sponsored by both of these groups went on.

Another way the British tried to settle the disturbances was to limit Jewish immigration and land purchase. In 1935 it is thought that over 60,000 Jews entered Palestine. (Precise figures are very hard to come by because Jewish figures underestimated the number of immigrants, Arab figures were overestimates, and British figures discounted the number of illegal immigrants.) This figure was halved in 1936 and further reduced in 1937 and 1938. It rose again to perhaps 30,000 in 1939, by which time dozens of new Jewish settlements had been established.

In 1939 British policy changed. Jewish immigration was cut back to about 4,000 a year and subsequent illegal immigrants were deported to Cyprus and Mauritius. In February 1940, huge areas of Palestine were set apart in which no further Jewish settlement was permitted. An independent Palestine, shared between Arab and Jew, was planned for 1949. The British had, in essence, washed their hands of the problem, although they undertook to police the region until the new state came into being. Their previous actions had alienated the Arabs. The new proposals, particularly in view of the plight of the Jews in Continental Europe, now alienated Jewish communities in Palestine and elsewhere.

ISRAEL

The independent Palestine that Britain had in mind was never founded. At the close of World War II there was mounting pressure from the United States (where the American Jews were successful in organizing themselves politically) and from Jewish terrorists in Palestine for the British to relax their immigration policy. Weakened and impoverished by the war, Britain invited the United States to participate in a committee of enquiry into the postwar plight of the Jews. The committee recommended that Palestine immigration limitations be lifted. The British government hesitated. The Arabs, speaking through the newly-formed Arab League, rejected the report.

As a result of a vote by the United Nations General Assembly, the new state of Israel was proclaimed in May 1948. Note how close Tel Aviv is to the eastern border.

On February 14, 1947, the British foreign secretary announced that Arab objections prevented a partition of Palestine and the mandate could not be governed as it then stood. Consequently, he was handing over the Palestinian problem to the United Nations. On August 21, 1947, the majority of a UN committee of enquiry recommended that Palestine be divided along the lines suggested by the Peel Commission of 1936–37. The plan was accepted by the General Assembly of the UN on November 29, carried by thirty-three votes to thirteen. The United States and the Soviet Union voted in favor, Britain against. The Jews adopted the name Israel for their new homeland.

The Arabs viewed this solution as the last straw in their struggle to make Palestine an independent Arab

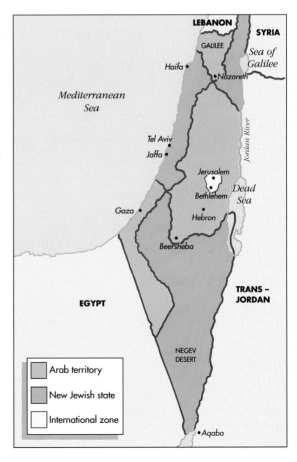

LEBANON
SYRIA
GALILEE
Sea of Galilee
Haifa
Nazareth
Mediterranean Sea
Jordan River
Tel Aviv
Jaffa
Jerusalem
Dead Sea
Bethlehem
Gaza
Hebron
Beersheba
TRANS – JORDAN
EGYPT
NEGEV DESERT

Arab territory
New Jewish state
International zone

Aqaba

Jewish refugees disembark at the port of Haifa in 1947 after their ship has been intercepted by British destroyers. Jewish organizations in the United States and Palestine urged the British to relax their immigration policy in the period leading up to the creation of Israel.

It is the natural right of the Jewish people to lead, as do all other nations, an independent existence in their sovereign State. Accordingly we, the members of the National Council representing the Jewish people in Palestine . . . hereby proclaim the establishment of the Jewish State in Palestine, to be called Medinath Yisrael (the State of Israel).

From the State of Israel Declaration of Independence, May 14, 1948.

state. Not surprisingly, they rejected the idea of an imposed partition. As the future Palestinian leader Yasir Arafat was to claim: "The Assembly [of the UN] partitioned what it had no right to divide — an indivisible homeland."

In the months before partition dozens of Britons, Jews, and Arabs were killed. As the British evacuated a town, Jews and Arabs fought to gain control over it. Thousands of Palestinian Arabs fled to neighboring Arab states. By 1948 units from the regular armies of Egypt, Syria, and Iraq were involved. When the state of Israel came into being in May 1948, it was simultaneously attacked by the armies of Lebanon, Syria, Iraq, Transjordan, Saudi Arabia, and Egypt.

The modern Arab-Israeli conflict had officially begun.

CONCLUSION

The causes of the Arab-Israeli conflict were deep-rooted and hard to deal with. They included the rise of nationalism among both the Jewish and Arab peoples, misguided and contradictory British statements made during World War I, uncertain government of the Palestinian mandate between the wars, and the wave of sympathy for the Jewish cause which followed the horrific anti-Semitic policies of the Nazis. To these may be added Jewish insensitivity toward Arab fears, the unwillingness of the Arabs to compromise, and the heavy-handed action of the United Nations in pressing ahead with partition in the face of Arab and British opposition.

Could the conflict have been prevented? No historical event is inevitable. Had courageous people from either side met, determined to solve the problem peaceably, a compromise might have been found. That is, after all, what eventually began to happen. But there were no such leaders at the time. And the longer the problem dragged on, the more deeply entrenched each side became. In the end, it took thirty years of bloodshed to move them.

Israel's first prime minister, David Ben-Gurion, (center left, in jacket) watches as the last British troops leave from the port of Haifa in July 1948.

AND SO TO WAR

The first and most obvious consequence of the Arab-Israeli conflict was war, and with war came death, destruction, homelessness, and misery.

In a sense it is not strictly accurate to divide the military conflict between Arab and Israeli into separate wars, because no Arab state made peace with Israel until the Camp David Agreement of 1978 formally ended hostilities between Egypt and Israel. Nevertheless, although there was a perpetual state of war from 1948 to 1978 (and beyond for most Arabs), the fighting flared into full-scale military conflict on only four occasions. These are described as the First, Second, Third, and Fourth Arab-Israeli Wars.

The frontiers of Israel in 1949 after the First Arab-Israeli War. The Israelis gained control over huge areas of new territory, but the Arabs held on to the West Bank and recaptured part of Jerusalem.

MAY 1948 — JULY 1949

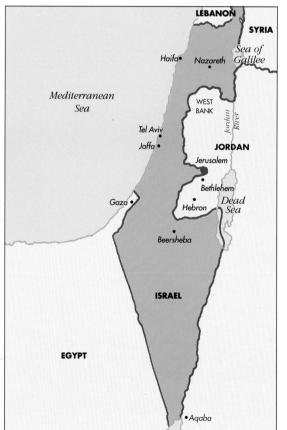

When the Arab armies moved against Israel in 1948, most observers, including the Arabs themselves, expected the new state to be swept off the map in months, if not weeks. Surprisingly, this did not happen. Not only did the Israelis resist the invasion, they also managed to drive back their assailants and capture large areas of Palestine. Six thousand Israelis and many more Arabs were killed in the fierce fighting.

Military historians now realize that Israeli success was not so surprising. The numbers of ground troops on either side were roughly similar. Although initially outgunned by their enemies, by 1949 the Israelis had managed to buy large quantities of modern arms and equipment from abroad. The Jewish Army was formed around the well-

Soldiers of the Israeli Haganah force on the way to Jerusalem, 1948. Every single member of the contingent was killed shortly after this picture was taken.

established Haganah. Their troops were experienced and knew the territory they were fighting in. Above all, they were fighting for survival. They had to win — if they did not, they and their families would be driven into the sea.

The Arab forces, on the other hand, were divided into separate, inexperienced armies under their own commanders operating with different battle plans. These problems, which bedeviled the Arabs in all their wars with Israel, reflected more fundamental difficulties. As the old mandate powers withdrew from the region after World War II, deep divisions emerged within the Arab world about how the Middle East should be organized. There were essentially three very different visions of what the Middle East should look like politically. One vision was Pan-Arabism. This was the somewhat ill-defined notion, arising out of the struggle for independence from the old imperial and colonial powers, that all Arabs should be united in a brotherhood reminiscent of the great days of Arab power that began in the seventh century. It found its most positive expression in the Arab League formed in March 1945 by the governments of Egypt, Iraq, Lebanon, Saudi Arabia, Syria, Transjordan, and Yemen. It was a loose association, intended to promote understanding and trade between the member states.

Pan-Arabism's principal difficulty was its inconsistency with the second vision of regional order: emerging nationalism, fostered by the governments of the separate, mostly newly-independent Arab states.

31

Understandably, member states tended to put their own interests before those of the wider group. The Arabs made separate truces with Israel between January and July 1949. Furthermore, Transjordan (renamed Jordan in 1949) and Egypt annexed the Palestinian lands not occupied by Israel. The disappearance of the Palestinian state was, therefore, completed by the Arabs' own actions. During the fighting there was always a fear that one Arab state might outperform the others, thereby increasing its own power at the expense of its neighbors'. For example, the Arab League refused to recognize Jordan's annexation of the Palestinian land on the west bank of the Jordan River. One of the expected consequences of the Arab-Israeli conflict was to widen the division between separate Arab nations, not to close it.

The third force or vision running through the Arab world was Pan-Islamism, or the call for all Muslims to unite against the infidel. In theory, this was a powerful sentiment for the Arab leaders to harness. But it was a double-edged sword. In Lebanon, where the population was divided between Christian and Muslim, it was to pull the country apart. Another problem was that the more popular Islamic leaders tended to be suspicious of Western technology and opposed to all-powerful secular governments. This led them into conflict with governments like that of the Saud family of Saudi Arabia, where fundamentalists rioted at the opening of the first television transmission center. Islamic fundamentalism's greatest triumph, bringing down the authori-

Some of the 800,000 Arab refugees created by the war of 1948–49 receiving medical aid from the Red Cross in the Palestinian village of Jiziya.

The beginning of years of exile and hardship — Palestinian refugee children at a makeshift school in a Jordanian camp, 1949.

tarian, secular regime of the Shah of Iran in 1979, was a stern warning to all governments in the Middle East. The fundamentalist-moderate split divided the Palestinian Liberation Organization, which represented the Palestinian cause, and destabilized Arab states, such as Egypt.

THE CONSEQUENCES OF WAR

The consequences of the First Arab-Israeli War set the character of the region for the rest of the century. It confirmed the existence of the state of Israel, although this was not recognized by the Arabs. Israel came into being with no fixed boundaries. The war expanded the territory under Israeli control by about a quarter. To the southeast it stretched to the port of Elat on the Gulf of Aqaba. From here the frontier ran north to the Mediterranean, along the boundary of the old Palestinian mandate. At the coast Egypt took over the Gaza Strip. In the north Israel's frontier was divided from Syria by the Golan Heights. To the east a large area on the west bank of the Jordan River remained in Arab hands. These frontiers were guaranteed by Britain, France, and the United States in 1950.

The war had serious consequences for Israel. Around 4,000 Jewish soldiers and 2,000 Jewish civilians were killed during this first war. It became a country on a permanent war footing, maintaining one of the world's largest armies in proportion to population and spending about 20 percent of its wealth on the armed forces. Although assisted by substantial foreign investment and aid, disproportionate military spending prevented the economy from expanding as it might have done under more peaceful conditions. Israel became a country under siege. Its citizens were subject to compulsory military service and grew up with a stern, siege mentality. Negotiations were frowned upon in case they were seen as signs of weakness, and hostility mounted toward all Arabs, both within and without their heavily defended frontiers.

If the consequences of the war were tough for Israel, they were even more so for millions of Palestinians. Thousands had been killed, both in the war and at the hands of Jewish terrorists. The United Nations estimated that 750,000 Palestinians fled from Israeli rule during 1948–49. Some found new homes and work, but many settled in the vast refugee camps established along Israel's borders. Because of the strain these refugees put on local resources, they were not always welcome. Those who found jobs and worked hard also became objects of scorn among their fellow Arabs. "The Jews of the Arab World" was one description given to them.

The Arabs left behind in Israel fared little better. Here they were second-class citizens in a country striving to promote its Jewishness. The Israelis declared that the Arabs within their frontiers had a higher standard of living than that enjoyed in many other Arab countries. However, this was scant consolation to a people who believed they were living in a land stolen from them by outsiders.

The war had consequences for the wider Arab world, too. It increased Arab suspicion of the United States, which had recognized the state of Israel the day it was formed. Defeat in the war of 1948–49 hastened the downfall of King Farouk of Egypt and the passage of power into the hands of extreme nationalists.

Finally, the most dangerous consequence of the First Arab-Israeli War was an Arab determination to seek revenge for their humiliation. Far from solving the problem of Palestine, the war had only made it worse.

The Palestine problem is the story of a people who lived peacefully in their own homes for generations. Then along came total strangers across the sea who turned the people out of their country and occupied their homes.

S. Hadawi, an Arab writer, cited in Walter Oppenheim, The Middle East, *Blackwell, 1989*

PLAYERS IN A WIDER GAME

THE COLD WAR

During World War II the Communist Soviet Union and democratic capitalist United States had fought together as uneasy allies. From 1943 onward, when it was looking increasingly likely that the Axis powers (Nazi Germany, Italy, and Japan) would be defeated, the Soviet and American governments started considering the postwar world. In conferences held at Yalta (February 1945) and Potsdam (June 1945) the two superpowers came to provisional agreements about each other's sphere of influence. This accord did not last. Neither side understood or trusted the other, and by 1947 they were in serious opposition. Both built up huge stockpiles of weapons and tried to outdo the other in attracting friends and allies around the world. The era of the Cold War had begun.

The "Big Three" at the Yalta Conference, February 1945 — (left to right) Soviet premier Joseph Stalin, United States President Franklin D. Roosevelt, and British prime minister Winston Churchill. Allied accord did not survive long after the war, and the Middle East became a central focus for the U.S.-Soviet Cold War.

The Suez Canal in 1951, an essential link in the route that supplied oil from the Middle East to the West. When Nasser came to power in 1952 he was determined to reclaim the canal from the British, who maintained a military presence in the area.

Wherever there was open conflict, the Soviets and the Americans watched carefully to see whether they might take advantage of the situation. The Arab-Israeli conflict drew their attention to the Middle East. To begin with they adopted similar positions, supporting the United Nations resolution calling for the partition of Palestine and the establishment of the state of Israel. American Jews sent funds to the Israelis, while the Soviets allowed Israel to purchase arms. In the 1950s, however, events in Egypt put an end to this understanding and set the superpowers against each other in the Middle East. Outside backing deepened and intensified the Arab-Israeli conflict, while also fueling the hostility of the Cold War.

THE SECOND ARAB-ISRAELI WAR

The military coup that toppled the Egyptian monarchy in 1952 eventually brought to power Colonel Gamal Abdul Nasser (1918–1970). Nasser was a Pan-Arab nationalist. His aim was to free his country of foreigners (there were still British bases along the Suez Canal) and to lead the Arab world. To do this, he was prepared to play off the United States against the Soviet Union.

Before Nasser came to power, American policy in the Middle East had been quite successful. The United States had appeased the Arabs by refusing to sell arms to Israel; and also sponsored an anti-Communist union, known as the Baghdad Pact, comprising Turkey, Pakistan, Iraq, Iran, and Britain. Nasser refused to join the Pact. Instead, in September 1955 he came to an agreement with the Soviets to exchange cotton for Czechoslovakian arms. In the eyes of the world the Soviet Union was now seen as the defender of Arab nationalism against the West. The Cold War had come to the Middle East.

The United States tried to get Nasser back into its camp by offering $50 million to fund his massive Aswan Dam project on the Nile River. It also put pressure on him by agreeing to France selling NATO arms to Israel. When Nasser refused to play the Americans' game, they withdrew funding for the Aswan Dam in July 1956. In response, Nasser nationalized the Suez Canal, saying he would use its revenues to pay for the dam. The action made him an Arab hero. Shivers of consternation ran through the Western world — the canal was a vital route for the supply of oil from the Middle East.

Britain, France, and Israel — but not the United States — decided to intervene. Tension had been mounting along the border between Egypt and Israel, and on October 29 the Israelis launched a full-scale attack. The next day, having secretly planned the operation with Israel beforehand, Britain and France attacked Egypt. First they bombed military targets, and then sent in

HANDS OFF EGYPT
In defiance of the UN charter and the principles of international law, the Anglo-French imperialists have launched an intervention against the independent Egyptian Republic in an attempt to seize by armed force the Suez Canal.

Report in the Soviet newspaper Pravda, *November 2, 1956*

Troops of the Anglo-French invasion force in Port Said, Egypt, in 1956. Without American backing, the European assault proved a costly embarrassment.

troops to seize the Suez Canal. Although Israel, Britain, and France achieved their military objective, the Egyptians had blocked the canal before it was taken and it remained shut for many months.

For a few tense days, with the Soviet Union threatening to intervene unless the aggressors withdrew, it looked as if the conflict might expand into a global one. United States forces went on standby. Fortunately, the Soviet Union was taken up with an anti-Communist revolt in Hungary, and the United States had sufficient economic power to force Britain and France to abide by a United Nations resolution and withdraw. The Israelis followed suit the following year.

Full-scale war had been averted. Britain and France had been humiliated and Arab morale boosted. But with the interference of the superpowers in the Middle East, the Arab-Israeli conflict had taken a turn for the worse. And the Palestinian problem was as far from a solution as it had ever been.

THE SOVIETS AND THE AMERICANS

For many years the Middle East remained one of the regions where East-West confrontation was at its most dangerous. The course of events was extremely

Scuttled ships block the Suez Canal, 1956. This move by the Egyptians rendered ineffective the Anglo-French seizure of the canal a short while later.

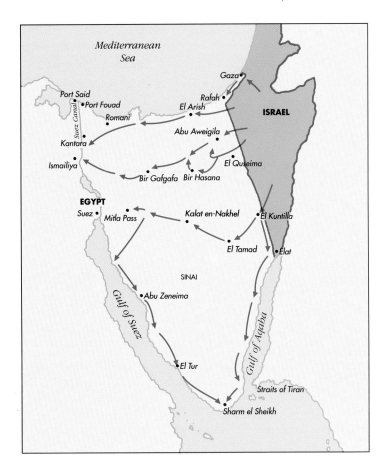

The lines of Israel's attack on Egypt, which began on October 29, 1956. By November 5, Sinai was in Israeli hands. At the same time, British and French troops seized the Suez Canal.

complex, with a bewildering series of wars, coups, and treaties following one another in quick succession. The Arabs were rarely united, and the activities of the superpowers (the United States and the Soviet Union) made a solution to the region's problems more difficult to achieve, at least until the later 1970s.

The diplomatic maneuvering of the superpowers added to the general problems of the Middle East. In the 1960s, for example, the Soviet Union engaged in a massive anti-Zionist campaign among the Arabs. This was not done for reasons of principle, but to unite the Arabs against the United States' ally, Israel. It served only to increase tension in the area. It may also be argued that the Soviet Union precipitated the Third War (1967) by leaking a warning to Egypt that its ally Syria was about to be attacked by Israel, and by telling the Egyptians that it would keep the United States in check if war broke out. The Soviet Union alone was not to blame. The Americans pursued their interests in the area just as ruthlessly. It is rumored that the United States was behind the coups in Syria

Cold War spin-off — British troops examine Soviet-made rocket launchers captured from the Egyptians, 1956.

If there is indeed a danger of nuclear confrontation in the Middle East, it would be enormously increased by a guaranteed settlement, which would involve the guarantors [the United States and the Soviet Union] in every border incident.

Bernard Lewis, The Great Powers, the Arabs and the Israelis, New York, 1969

(1961) and Iraq (1963) that temporarily removed those countries from the Soviet sphere of influence.

The primary manner in which the United States and the Soviet Union fueled the Arab-Israeli conflict was by supplying arms to either side. As we have seen, the process began in 1955 with Nasser's agreement to obtain arms from Czechoslovakia and the United States' response of agreeing to France supplying Israel. The year after the Suez crisis the United States Congress launched its "Eisenhower Doctrine," promising arms to any Middle East power seeking to resist communism.

It has been estimated that between 1968 and 1973 the Soviet Union stocked the Arabs with arms worth $2.5 billion, while over the same period the United States provided Israel with weapons worth about half that sum, as well as economic aid worth $420 million. By the end of 1970 there were 20,000 Soviet military advisors in Egypt. These were soon joined by Soviet pilots flying Egyptian aircraft. The weapons enabled Arabs and Israelis to engage in a Fourth Arab-Israeli War (1973). The weapons lost in this war were soon replaced, the Egyptians and Syrians reportedly receiving $4 billion worth of Soviet arms in 1974, including Scud missiles. Sources say that in the same year the

Israelis bought arms from the United States to the value of $1.5 billion. A refusal to provide arms to Israel and the Arabs (if such a move had been feasible) would not really have solved the Palestinian question, but it might have made both sides less ready to resort to war.

Another consequence of United States-Soviet involvement in the Arab-Israeli conflict was that on occasion it brought the world close to nuclear disaster. In 1967 the Soviet Union said it would intervene militarily in the war, even launching rockets against Britain and France, unless the Israeli advance was stopped. There was a similar crisis over Jordan in 1970 and again during the Fourth War (1973), when all Soviet airborne divisions were held on standby and the American armed forces put on global alert. Only last-minute compromise prevented the Arab-Israeli conflict from having the most ghastly consequence of all.

President Nasser of Egypt (center) with Soviet leader Nikita Khrushchev (left) and President Tito of Yugoslavia (right) in 1960. The supply of arms from the Soviet Union and the United States enabled Arabs and Israelis to continue their bitter fight for Palestine.

THE THIRD AND FOURTH WARS

THE CONSEQUENCES OF THE SECOND ARAB-ISRAELI WAR

Moshe Dayan (1915–81), Israeli chief of staff in the Sinai War of 1956 and minister of defense during the Six-Day War of 1967. He is seen here in 1973 with General Ariel Sharon, who became minister of defense some years later.

The consequences of the Second Arab-Israeli War, also known as the Suez Crisis and the Sinai Campaign, rumbled around the world. The conflict confirmed the decline of Britain and France as great powers, which in turn meant that events in the Middle East would now be ever more dependent on the power plays of the two superpowers. During the Suez Crisis of 1956 the governments of the United States and the Soviet Union put their forces on alert, ready to intervene if events took a turn which they found unacceptable.

Another unfortunate result of the war was to reveal once again the weakness of the United Nations. Throughout the Arab-Israeli conflict, the UN passed resolutions, patrolled frontiers, and arranged cease-fires. But it was always reacting to events rather than controlling them. Unless its two most powerful members, the United States and the Soviet Union, acted in agreement, the UN was essentially helpless.

By the end of 1956 Britain's humiliation was total, although it attempted to blame its failure on the United States' unwillingness to support its Western allies. Prime Minister Eden, his health shattered, resigned in January 1957. The blocking of the Suez Canal (closed until 1957) and an Arab cutback in oil supplies led to gas rationing and economic hardship. Britain's remaining colonies, on the other hand, took heart at what had happened and increased their demands for independence.

The effects on France were similar. The Fourth Republic was further discredited, hastening its collapse in 1958. Encouraged by Egypt's success, France's Arab colonies in North Africa clamored for independence.

The consequences for Israel were, however, more mixed. With Egypt now firmly in the Soviet camp, Israel's dependence on the United States had increased. The Sinai Campaign had gone well for the Israelis, but without American backing they had been obliged to call it off and hand back all captured territory. Even so, they had won notable military successes. The port of Elat, subjected to an Egyptian blockade before the war, had been reopened to trade. Israeli military superiority had been confirmed and many Soviet-built Egyptian tanks captured for use in the Israeli Army. Finally, they had compelled Egypt to cancel the campaign by Palestinian terrorists.

In Arab eyes the war had been far more of a success than a failure. In the showdown with Britain and France, Nasser's prestige had risen to new heights. Despite another defeat at the hands of the Israelis, the Arab world was jubilant. In 1958 Egypt and Syria joined together to form the United Arab Republic, their union lasting until the Syrian coup of 1961. In Iraq the pro-British government was toppled, also in 1958, and the new regime welcomed massive quantities of Soviet weapons and aid. Nasser had divided Britain and France from the United States and succeeded in bringing about a degree of Arab unity.

Israeli forces advance through the Sinai as Egyptian prisoners are taken away by truck in the opposite direction, 1967.

Six years after the Second Arab-Israeli War the Arab nations around Israel's borders were well armed and confident. The Cold War dispute between the United States and Soviet Union confused issues in the Middle East. There was little incentive to try and resolve the complicated Arab-Israeli disputes through diplomacy. It seemed only a matter of time before war erupted again.

THE SIX-DAY WAR

The Third War, known as the Six-Day War or the June War, occurred in June 1967. The specific point of tension occurred along the border between Israel and Syria, where the Syrians attempted to divert the waters of the Jordan River and the Israelis resisted by force. Soviet scheming helped build up a war fever and Egypt's President Nasser played a dangerous game of threatening war without, it seems, actually intending to start one.

The Israeli minister of defense, Moshe Dayan, decided that if Israel was to avoid defeat, it had to strike first. On June 5 Israel launched a massive air strike against Egypt, virtually wiping out its air force.

Without air cover, the Egyptian ground forces were helpless, and within three days Israeli tanks had reached the Suez Canal. In the east, the Israelis drove the Jordanians back across the Jordan River, and by June 9 the Israeli Army controlled the Golan Heights in Syria and was on the road to Damascus. The United Nations call for a cease-fire was accepted by Jordan on June 7, and then by Egypt and Syria. By June 10 Israel had won one of the most remarkable victories in modern history.

In the short term the Six-Day War brought the Arab-Israeli conflict no nearer to a solution. The Israelis were too proud and confident after their victory, and the Arabs too bitter and humiliated by their defeat, to make serious peace negotiations realistic. Some 15,000 soldiers had been killed, the majority of them Arabs, and perhaps a million more Palestinians were now under Israeli rule in the Gaza Strip and the West Bank. Nevertheless, in the long run the war may have had consequences that contributed to the eventual solving of the Palestinian problem.

After the war in June Israel felt more secure behind easily defensible frontiers — the Suez Canal, the Jordan River, and the Golan Heights. For the first

The reality of war — a wounded Egyptian prisoner of war, stripped of his uniform, is supported by his comrades, 1967.

We will win because we must live. Our neighbors are fighting not for their lives, nor for their sovereignty. They are fighting to destroy us. We dare not be destroyed.

From a speech by Israel's prime minister, Golda Meir, October 13, 1973

The battlefields of the remarkable Six-Day War of 1967, when Israel captured Sinai and the key strategic areas of the Golan Heights, the West Bank, and the Gaza Strip.

time since 1948 the Israelis were in a strong position in relation to their Arab neighbors. There was hope that in exchange for the lands captured from Egypt, Jordan, and Syria, the Arabs would perhaps recognize Israel's right to exist.

The lesson of the 1967 war for many Arabs was the realization that they were unlikely ever to defeat their enemy in war. As a result, particularly after this opinion was confirmed in the 1973 war, certain Arab leaders began to consider the possibility of a negotiated settlement with Israel. A similar mood was reflected in the diplomacy of the superpowers, who agreed in 1972 to look for ways of defusing the tension in the Middle East.

Finally, the Six-Day War brought the plight of the Palestinians firmly before the eyes of the world. Friction between the Israelis and the much larger Palestinian Arab community now within their borders increasingly damaged the public image of Israel, as widespread sympathy for the hundreds of thousands of refugees crammed into squalid camps grew. The Palestinians also increasingly drew attention to their cause through a campaign of terrorism.

FIGHTING FOR PEACE

In 1969–70 President Nasser kept up the military pressure on Israel by conducting a war of attrition along the Suez Canal. His successor, Anwar Sadat (president of Egypt 1970–81), also realized that his country was unlikely to defeat Israel in the battlefield. He felt that only the superpowers had the means to bring the two sides together. First he tried rejecting the Soviets, in the hope that the United States would take their place as Egypt's supporter. When this did not happen, he determined to force the issue by showing the United States that the

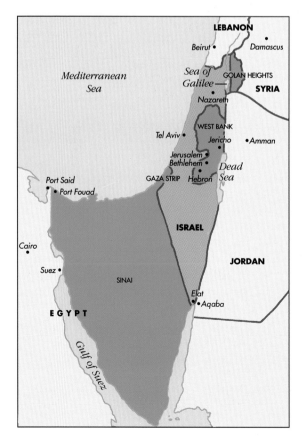

existing situation between Arabs and Israelis would never bring lasting peace or security. On October 6, 1973, in conjunction with his Syrian allies, he launched the Fourth Arab-Israeli War.

This war, known as the Yom Kippur War or the October War, achieved precisely the aim he had been seeking. By October 24, when a cease-fire was declared, the Israelis were once again driving into Arab territory. But this time their success had not come easily. They had been caught completely by surprise and driven back both on the Sinai peninsula and on the Golan Heights. The Israelis reversed these setbacks only at a very high cost in soldiers and equipment, and with substantial American aid. Sadat had erased the Arab humiliation after the 1967 war and had proved that the Arabs could still hurt Israel — and would continue to do so until a settlement was reached.

The Yom Kippur War demonstrated that the Arabs could hurt Israel's Western allies, too. To support the efforts of the armies in the field, the oil-producing Arab states placed an oil embargo on the United States and also reduced oil shipments to Western Europe. The Western economies were thrown into confusion by the sudden shortage of oil for their industrial economies. Now, at last, the Arabs had a weapon that would make the superpowers listen.

An Israeli soldier tends a wounded comrade during the Yom Kippur War of October 1973.

We have fought for the sake of peace, the only peace that really deserves to be called peace — peace based on justice. Our enemy sometimes speaks about peace. But there is a vast difference between the peace of aggression and the peace of justice.

President Sadat of Egypt in a speech to the People's Assembly, Cairo, October 16, 1973

THE PALESTINIANS

THE PALESTINIANS AND THE CAMPS

One of the most ironic consequences of the Arab-Israeli conflict was the way it reversed the fortunes of the Israelis and the Palestinians. Before the creation of Israel, the Jews were a people without a homeland. After 1948 many Palestinians found themselves refugees.

A Palestinian refugee camp in Jordan, 1971. Israelis claimed that if the oil-rich Arab states had the political will, they could end the poverty of the Palestinian refugees in a matter of months.

Estimates of the number of Palestinians living within the frontiers of Israel vary widely, with the Arabs generally exaggerating the figures and the Israelis underestimating them. However, in 1982 it was thought that the Palestinian population in Israel, including the West Bank, Gaza Strip, and East Jerusalem, stood at approximately 1,800,000.

In 1989 the United Nations Relief Works Agency estimated the numbers of Palestinians living in refugee camps as follows:

Country	Number of camps	Refugees in camps
Lebanon	13	148,809
Syria	10	75,208
Israel - West Bank	19	373,586
- Gaza Strip	8	244,416
Jordan	10	208,716
Total	60	**1,050,735**

The conditions in these camps were generally very poor. Men, women, and children lived in rotting tents and makeshift housing, and were fed with United Nations rations. They had to endure poor education facilities, water shortages, and unemployment. They were exploited by terrorist groups. After a visit to the camps in 1988, the British Labour Party leader described them as "hell."

The soldiers of tomorrow — Palestinian children of the al-Fatah movement being trained in the art of war.

By the late 1980s the Palestinians living in the West Bank and Gaza began to take matters into their own hands by declaring an *intifada* or uprising against the Israeli occupation force. Beginning in the Gaza Strip and soon spreading to the West Bank, the *intifada* started with stone-throwing at Israeli police and security forces. Before long the violence had escalated to the use of knives, guns, and bombs. There was trouble among Palestinians, too, as the radicals killed those suspected of collaborating with the Israelis.

The Israeli authorities were uncertain about how to deal with the *intifada*. Their soldiers were trained in warfare, not riot control. On occasion — often in full view of the world's media — they overreacted with beatings, and with the use of tear gas, rubber bullets, and live ammunition on the Palestinians. Since the victims of these strong-arm tactics by the Israeli military were invariably young people, usually groups of boys gathered on street corners, the international reaction was one of outrage. Israeli figures suggest that by 1991, 697 Palestinians —78 of whom were under fourteen years old — had been killed by the Israeli Army and 13,967 Palestinians had been wounded. Over the same period 13 members of the Israeli

The 1993 PLO-Israeli accord gave the Palestinians a degree of self-government in the Gaza Strip, but it did not end the strife and bitterness there. Here, in 1994, Palestinian soldiers try to stop a stone-throwing mob at the main Palestinian crossing point between Israel and the Strip.

security forces and 12 civilians had been killed by the Palestinians, and the corresponding figures for the wounded were 3,000 and 1,268.

One of the major problems in reaching a long-term solution to the Palestinian refugee problem was that both sides shrugged off responsibility for them. The Arab states never failed to point out that the refugees were the product of Israeli conquest. In response, the Israelis claimed that the Arabs allowed the terrible conditions in the camps to continue for political reasons instead of absorbing the refugees into their own populations. The Israelis also accused the Arab regimes of using the camps to evoke sympathy for their cause. The camps also provided a ready recruiting ground for Palestinian terrorists, and

One young Palestinian rescues another who has been wounded in the riots of March 2, 1994.

were even used as terrorist bases. Moreover, the Israelis pointed out that they gave as much to the Palestinian Refugee Fund as any Arab state, and they argued that one day's Arab oil revenues could have solved the problem overnight. The Arab reply was that the Palestinian right to their homeland was not for sale.

THE PALESTINIAN LIBERATION ORGANIZATION

The Palestinians were much slower to develop an effective nationalist movement than were the Zionists. In part this was due to the fact that, as subjects of the Ottoman Empire for centuries, they were not so familiar with the tactics of modern nation-building.

At first, their leader, at least officially, was the grand mufti of Jerusalem, the senior Muslim religious authority in Palestine. In 1949 he set himself up in Gaza as head of the All Palestine Government, and encouraged terrorism by various groups of *fedayeen* (meaning, literally, those who are willing to sacrifice their lives to a cause). The grand mufti was not an effective commander. His credibility with Western leaders was limited because he had lived in Nazi Germany from 1942–45.

Some Palestinian groups operated independently of the grand mufti. In 1964 the Egyptians encouraged the formation of the Palestine Liberation Organization

The grand mufti of Jerusalem with Adolf Hitler during World War II. The mufti lived in Nazi Germany from 1942 to 1945, a fact which did little to help the Arab cause gain favor in the West.

(PLO) to coordinate all the Palestinian groups in their efforts to drive the Israelis from Palestine. The PLO's Charter called for a "democratic and secular Palestine" and for the "elimination" of the state of Israel. By the end of 1969 the PLO was operating from Jordan under the chairmanship of Yasir Arafat.

The PLO was never more than a large, loosely organized association, containing factions such as the radical Popular Front for the Liberation of Palestine and the Democratic Front for the Liberation of Palestine, as well as the more moderate groups like al-Fatah. Not all members of the PLO were guerrillas either — many were professional people who did not participate in violent actions. Jordan initially served as the base for PLO military attacks against Israel. In 1970 tension between the government of King Hussein and the PLO led to civil war in Jordan and ultimately to the expulsion of the PLO to Lebanon and Syria. Even so, the PLO continued to grow in importance and authority. In October 1974 a meeting of Arab governments formally recognized the PLO as the only authority that could speak on behalf of all Palestinians. The

No one is safe. The wrecked interior of the Israeli school bus in which eight children and three adults were killed in a Palestinian bazooka attack, May 1970.

Al-Fatah, the largest and most moderate of the Palestinian resistance organizations, announced today that it was responsible for the guerrilla raid that resulted in seven deaths last night at the Israeli town of Nahariya.

The New York Times, *June 26, 1974*

organization was recognized soon after by the United Nations, and recognition by the governments of other nations followed. But the crucial recognition — that of Israel — was still a long way off, and this hampered attempts at Arab-Israeli talks on a settlement of the Palestinian problem.

In the Western world, however, the PLO attracted attention principally for its acts of terrorism. The great majority of its terrorist activities were directed against Israel. In 1976, for example, terrorist bombs killed eight Israelis in Jerusalem, while on March 11, 1978, a group of Palestinian war guerrillas landed on the coast north of Tel Aviv, hijacked a holiday bus, and killed thirty-nine Israelis.

Even more outrageous, as far as international opinion was concerned, were the attacks made on civilians outside Israel, many of whom had only the slightest links with Palestine's enemies. Often the culprits were found not to be members of the mainstream PLO but of extremist splinter groups, such as Black September. Airplanes and airports were the primary targets. In September 1970 the PLO hijacked four airliners, held 600 passengers hostage, and destroyed three airplanes on the ground in Jordan. Two years later they received a ransom of $5 million for a hijacked German airliner, and killed eleven Israeli athletes in a raid on the Munich Olympic Games. Similar acts continued throughout the 1970s and 1980s. Despite much tighter security, only occasionally were the security forces able to turn the tables on the terrorists. The best known example occurred in 1976, when a French airplane with 258 people on board was hijacked to Entebbe in Uganda. Israeli special forces followed it there and launched a raid in which they freed the hostages and killed the terrorists.

Was terrorism justified? Most people would argue that not only was it morally evil but it also harmed the Palestinian cause by turning world opinion against it. The terrorists countered this by saying that the world ignored their plight until they engaged in these violent acts. Some terrorists argued that their terrorism was in response to the greatest act of terrorism of all, namely, turning over Palestine to the Israelis. The way to stop Palestinian terrorism, they reasoned, was for the Jews to hand back Palestine to its rightful owners. Whether these arguments were valid or not, terrorist activity certainly served to keep the Palestinian issue in the headlines.

These criminal acts of hijacking planes, of detaining passengers, of blowing up aircraft are deplorable and must be condemned. It is high time we adopted effective measures to put a stop to this retreat to the law of the jungle.

The Secretary-General of the United Nations, cited in Walter Oppenheim, The Middle East, *1989*

THE CHAOS SPREADS

RIPPLES OF INSTABILITY

Throughout its long history the Arab-Israeli conflict sent ripples of political instability across the Middle East and far beyond. As we have seen, the First Arab-Israeli War in 1948 was partly responsible for the fall of Egypt's king Farouk in 1952. The war over Suez in 1956 led, directly or indirectly, to the resignation of the British prime minister, Anthony Eden, and the collapse of France's Fourth Republic. In 1973 the United States and the Soviet Union put their armed forces on maximum alert. The formation of the United Arab Republic and its subsequent collapse following the coup in Syria (1958–61) make sense only in the context of the Palestinian situation.

Within Israel itself the state of almost continual war with the Arabs had important effects on national politics. From 1948 to 1977 the country was dominated

A Shiite militiaman fires a deadly rocket propelled grenade at Palestinians in the Sabra refugee camp, Lebanon, 1986. The spread of the Arab-Israeli conflict into the unstable cultural mix of modern Lebanon was one of the conflict's more tragic consequences.

by the Labor Party, led by Prime Ministers David Ben-Gurion (1948–53 and 1955–63), Levi Eshkol (1963–69), Golda Meir (1969–74), and Yitzhak Rabin (1974–77). By the end of the 1960s the strain of living in a state of siege had begun to undermine Labor's power. In 1977 the Likud, a right-wing alliance, came to power under Prime Minister Menachem Begin. Partly in response to mounting terrorism, Jewish settlers moved into the West Bank and onto the Golan Heights, making a future agreement with Jordan and Syria more difficult. A Labor-Likud alliance under Shimon Peres (1984–86) and Yitzhak Shamir (1986–92) reflected the way the country was divided — one side (Labor) willing to accept a negotiated settlement with the Palestinians; the other, typified by Shamir, unwilling even to recognize the PLO's existence. Although Rabin's 1993 accord with Yasir Arafat was backed by the majority of Israelis, there remained a minority opposed to any negotiations with the PLO.

In Jordan the Israeli-Palestinian conflict had even more dire consequences, throwing the country into civil war. King Hussein had always favored negotiated settlement with Israel. He was displeased, therefore, when the PLO began using Jordan as a base for their

Russian-born Golda Meir (center) came to Palestine in 1921. She was prime minister of Israel 1969–74, and is seen here with U.S. secretary of state Henry Kissinger and Mrs. Kissinger near the end of her period in office.

terrorist activities. In time they set up what was virtually a state within a state. The crisis came in 1970, when Egypt halted its war of attrition with Israel and the PLO determined to continue the struggle through terrorism. When three Western aircraft were blown up at Amman airport, Hussein declared martial law and moved against the Palestinians.

The arrival in September of Syrian tanks to help the Palestinians escalated a civil war into an international crisis. If Jordan fell to the PLO and the Syrians, Israel would be surrounded by countries allied to the Soviet Union. The United States put its armed forces on alert. Hussein asked the British, Americans, and Israelis for help. President Richard Nixon informed Hussein that the United States would come to his assistance if the Jordanians were not able to halt the Syrians on their own. Although the Soviets were urging restraint on the Syrians, they could not afford to be seen to back down under American pressure. Fortunately, the Jordanian Army managed to repel the invaders, and the Palestinians were soon driven from Jordan. A major East-West conflict had been narrowly averted.

The explosion of terrorism — Palestinian terrorists destroy a hijacked British VC10 airplane at Amman airport, Jordan in 1970. Unsuccessful on the battlefield, the Palestinians turned to terrorism to draw the world's attention to their cause.

CAMP DAVID ACCORDS

The October War (1973) had once again brought the United States and the Soviet Union close to open conflict. It was now clear that it was in neither of their interests to continue the confrontation between Israel

The March 1979 signing of a Middle East peace treaty agreed to in the Camp David Accords of 1978. Arranged by President Carter (center), the accord between Egypt's president Anwar Sadat (left) and Israeli prime minister Menachem Begin (right) finally broke the Middle East stalemate. Two years later Sadat was assassinated by Arab extremists.

and its Arab neighbors. Through American mediation, Israel and Egypt signed an armistice on November 11, 1973. When a UN-sponsored conference between Egypt, Jordan, the United States, and the Soviet Union failed to make much headway, the Egyptian president, Anwar Sadat, suggested that the United States should continue to mediate between his country and Israel in an attempt to bring a permanent end to their hostilities. The Soviet leaders might have tried to stop the process, but decided instead to stand aside. They were forced to concede to growing American dominance in the region.

In 1974 the United States arranged disengagement agreements between Israel, Syria, and Egypt. When Egypt continued the process the following year, setting up a wide buffer zone along the Sinai border, other Arab states grew suspicious. President Jimmy Carter tried to calm their worries by suggesting a general Middle East settlement. This idealistic proposal came to nothing, but President Sadat refused to let the peace process stop. In 1977 he startled the whole world by offering to go to Jerusalem in person and address the Knesset, the Israeli parliament.

Sadat's move was greeted with delight everywhere but in the hard-line Arab states. President Carter became involved in the discussions and in September

1978 Sadat and Begin signed a momentous series of accords at Camp David, the President's country retreat outside Washington, D.C. These agreements stated that Egypt and Israel would recognize each other, exchange ambassadors, and sign a formal peace treaty. Sinai would be returned to Egypt in stages, and Israeli ships would be free to use the Suez Canal and the Gulf of Aqaba. The plight of the Palestinians was not dealt with directly, although Begin agreed to work toward limited self-government for the Gaza Strip and the West Bank.

Those who hoped the Camp David Accords would soon lead to a general peace in the region were disappointed. Most Arab states condemned Sadat as a traitor and Egypt was expelled from the Arab League. Yet, in October 1981, when Sadat was assassinated by Muslim extremists, the Arab world lost one of its most visionary leaders.

THE MISERY OF LEBANON

No country has felt the consequences of the Arab-Israeli conflict more heavily than Lebanon. With a delicate balance of Christian and Muslim populations,

Terrified Christian Lebanese wait in their bullet-riddled car to cross divided Beirut during the civil war in Lebanon.

The wretchedness of Lebanon's civil war caught in the anguish of a Muslim woman whose home has just been destroyed, 1989. The painting on the wall is of her son, killed in fight-ing five years before.

During the past nine weeks, we have, in effect, destroyed the combat potential of 20,000 terrorists. We hold 9,000 in a prison camp. Between 2,000 and 3,000 were killed and between 7,000 and 9,000 have been captured and cut off in Beirut. They have decided to leave there only because they have no possi-bility of remaining there. The problem will be solved.

From a speech by Prime Minister Menachem Begin, August 8, 1982

Lebanon was destabilized by developments farther south. Yet for many years, despite its border with Israel, Lebanon managed to remain comparatively unharmed by the conflict. It was neutral during the four wars, although the 1956 crisis opened up such deep divisions that by 1958 American troops had come in to prevent the possibility of civil war. By the time of the last war, however, the situation was changing fast.

The principal reason why Lebanon was drawn into the Arab-Israeli struggle was the arrival in the coun-try of the PLO after its expulsion from Jordan in 1970. The story then became so complicated that not even the Lebanese themselves always knew what was going on. The Christians split into moderate and militant factions. The Muslims became infinitely more divided,

both by sect and politics. All groups were funded and
supplied with weapons by outsiders, notably by Libya.
The situation was further troubled by the presence in
Lebanon of both Syrians and Israelis. Large areas of
the once beautiful and prosperous city of Beirut — "the
Paris of the Middle East" — were smashed and
burned. The Lebanese and the Palestinian refugees
were brutalized by the conflict.

The civil war in Lebanon began in 1975, triggered
by the massacre of a busload of Palestinians. Syria
sent in troops the following year and the Israelis
entered in 1978. Peacekeeping efforts by the United
Nations failed, and the Israelis invaded a second time
in 1982, driving the PLO from the country. The month
following the PLO's departure a pro-Israeli Lebanese
Christian faction carried out a terrible massacre of
Palestinians in the Sabra and Chatila refugee camps,
close to Beirut. The Israelis, who controlled the area
around the camps and had done nothing to stop the
killing of an estimated 2,000 men, women, and children, were held responsible by much of the world's
community. In response to the carnage, the United
Nations sent in a multinational peace force. It too

*Palestinians
emerge from Bourj
Al-Barajneh
refugee camp near
Beirut in 1988.
The camp was
destroyed during
a seige that lasted
three years.*

Rescuers search through the remains of the bombed head-quarters of the United States Marines, Beirut, October 1983.

failed to hold the warring sides apart, and pulled out shortly after a suicide bomber had blown up a United States Marine base, killing 241 people. A similar attack on French troops left fifty-nine dead.

Following the withdrawal of the United Nations forces, Lebanon deteriorated into a nightmare of fighting and hostage taking, with the Syrians and Israelis intervening from time to time to support their own interests. Two developments finally brought the tragedy to a halt. One was the end of the Cold War; the other was the Taif Accord, a peace plan prepared by the Arab League in October 1989 which allowed Syria to remain in occupation of Lebanon. By 1990 a shaky peace had returned to Lebanon and the people were beginning to rebuild their shattered country. Nevertheless, the situation remained uncertain as sporadic fighting continued between the Israelis and Muslim guerrilla groups (such as the *Hezbollah*) based in the south of the country.

THE WORLD'S PROBLEM

THE UNITED NATIONS

Although the United Nations was deeply involved in the Israeli-Palestinian conflict since the founding of that world body, none of its efforts to resolve the struggle led very far. In 1947 the UN appointed a mediator who was ultimately assassinated by Jewish extremists. The UN's weakness became even more apparent as the conflict continued. Although powerless to prevent the fighting in 1956, it arranged for the Suez Canal to be cleared, and sent its first peacekeeping force to stand between the opposing armies. The United Nations Emergency Force (UNEF) was deployed in the Sinai Peninsula, with Egyptian consent. When Egypt demanded the withdrawal of UNEF in May 1967, the force had to leave, thereby contributing to the Six-Day War.

Inside a barrack room in the Mia Mia camp, Lebanon, 1952. The camp was funded by the United Nations Relief and Works Agency for Palestinian Refugees. Unable to stop the violence, the UN concentrated its efforts on helping the conflict's victims.

This resolution comprises the liquidation of the Zionist existence, since the Palestine homeland is Palestine, and Palestine at present is Israel.

Yasir Arafat on the United Nations condemnation of Zionism, in Al-Balagh, *Beirut, January 5, 1975*

Palestinian refugee children receiving treatment in a United Nations hospital in Lebanon, 1961. The UN relief effort in the Middle East employed around 10,000 people, almost all of them Palestinians.

The United Nations again called for a cease-fire in 1967 and then went on to monitor it. Although the disengagement and subsequent settlement between Israel and Egypt after the 1973 War was largely arranged by American diplomacy, the UN proved a useful, neutral fourth party, and provided the forces required to police Israel's borders with Egypt and Syria. A pattern of the UN involvement in the conflict gradually emerged: there is generally an outbreak of violence, followed by a UN demand for a cease-fire and withdrawal, the disengagement of military forces and arrival of UN observers and peacekeepers, UN withdrawal, and then a fresh outbreak of violence.

The United Nations can resist aggression with armed force only when it has the unanimous support of its Security Council, as it did during the Gulf War of 1991. It never found such unanimity over the Arab-Israeli conflict. However, the Security Council endorsed UN Resolution 242 in 1967, calling for the withdrawal of Israeli troops from all territories occupied that year in exchange for a permanent peace. The land for peace formula became the basis for all later peace initiatives. From 1974 onward the PLO was granted observer status by the UN General

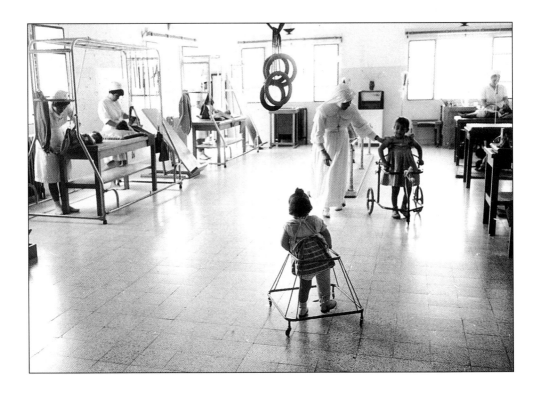

Assembly. On November 10, 1975, the General Assembly of the UN voted by a large majority to condemn Zionism as "a form of racism and racial discrimination." The General Assembly also set up the grandiose-sounding "United Nations Committee on the Exercise of the Inalienable Rights of the Palestinian People." The Committee's demands, and similar demands by other UN bodies, carried little weight with the Security Council and therefore remained largely just talk.

In one area the United Nations won the respect and thanks of all parties. This was its work for the care of Palestinian refugees. When no one else would take responsibility for them, the UN set up the United Nations Relief and Works Agency for Palestine Refugees in the Near East (UNRWA). Since its establishment in 1949, UNRWA has provided education, training, health care, and relief services to millions of Palestinians. By mid-1984 it was coping with over two million refugees and was running 635 refugee schools. Its annual budget, raised through voluntary contributions, was $231 million. Between 1950 and 1974 the United States gave $577 million, Britain gave

United Nations officers from Denmark and Canada, escorted by Israelis, inspect a cease-fire line in Syria, 1967. UN observers and peacekeepers monitored areas of conflict after the organization had demanded a cease-fire.

The horror goes on — United Nations peacekeepers pick through the wreckage of an Israeli-bombed house in the southern Lebanese village of Siddiqine, 1993.

$133 million, Israel, Saudi Arabia, and Egypt gave about $5 million each. The Soviet Union, the principal backer of the Arab cause, and the Arab state of Algeria made no contributions.

THE POWER OF OIL

By the second half of the twentieth century oil was the world's principal source of energy. It powered electricity generating stations, cars, trucks, domestic heating, and industry. By the 1960s over half the world's oil came from the Arab oil fields in Saudi Arabia, Iraq, Libya, and Algeria. Britain imported 63 percent of its oil from the Arabs, West Germany 74 percent, France 77 percent, and Italy 79 percent. Likewise, the majority of American oil imports came from the Middle East. It was only a matter of time before the Arabs exploited this dependence for political ends.

At a meeting of the Organization of Oil Exporting Countries (OPEC) in October 1973, in order to help Arab armies in the field, OPEC declared that it would (1) double the price of oil and continue to increase its price at regular intervals, (2) cut back production by five percent a month until Israel withdrew from occupied territories, and (3) stop all exports to countries directly supporting Israel. The resultant economic chaos was one of the principal consequences of the Arab-Israeli conflict.

The price of fuel soared, feeding inflation and economic and political disruption. The United States, Israel's most powerful ally and the leader of the world economy, was hard hit. The country was already having to cope with the loss of South Vietnam to the Communists. There was also great concern over the Watergate crisis which eventually led to President Nixon's resignation in August 1974. Inflation and stagnation — "stagflation" — struck the American economy. Fights broke out in the long lines at gas stations as motorists waited to buy fuel. The auto industry in the United States, which for years had produced cars with little concern for the cost of gas, now found itself undercut by fuel-efficient imports from Japan and Europe. It was against this background that American diplomats, notably Secretary of State Henry Kissinger, shuttled back and forth across the Middle East in an attempt to find a lasting solution to the Middle East crisis.

Oil, the Arabs' greatest weapon, was employed with devastating effect in 1973 when OPEC decided to double its prices and cut production. This caused widespread economic and political problems in the United States and Europe.

Europe was hit just as hard. British industry went on a three-day working week, inflation rose to 25 percent and the Conservative government of Edward Heath was defeated at two elections in 1974. Similar, though less drastic effects were felt by the other industrialized nations.

Eventually the oil weapon began to lose its sharpness as oil dependent countries developed alternative sources of energy, such as solar and nuclear power, and launched energy-saving campaigns. Other sources of oil were exploited, particularly in the Far East and the North Sea. And the Arab oil producers found that by crippling the world economy they were destroying the basis of their own prosperity — the poorer a country became, the less oil it required. Moreover, the conservative Arab oil-producing states, particularly Saudi Arabia, realized that by weakening the West they were playing into the hands of the Communist bloc, which had no liking for absolutist monarchies, however kind and generous. By 1982 oil prices had returned to their 1972 levels and the crisis was over. Having played their strongest card, the Arabs had still not won the game. The Arab-Israeli conflict rumbled on.

Fuel crisis, 1974. Oil shortages brought pressure on the West to reduce its support for Israel, and forced angry motorists to wait for hours to buy gas.

TOWARD A NEW WORLD

CONSEQUENCES OF CONFLICT—
A SUMMARY

The Arab-Israeli wars since 1945 were the most serious regional conflicts during the Cold War. The most obvious and unpleasant result of these wars was an unending list of human misery. This included the thousands of soldiers killed and maimed in war and the grief caused to their families, and the equally large number of civilian casualties of air and ground raids, including victims of terrorism. To these may be added the shattered lives of refugees, both Palestinian and Lebanese.

The material devastation caused by the conflict was enormous. Each war saw hundreds of burned out tanks and other vehicles, aircraft destroyed, and buildings shattered. Bombs and artillery fire left parts of Beirut looking like a ghost city.

Coupled to the material destruction was the waste of financial resources channeled into the war effort. Israel, for example, was spending almost a quarter of its wealth on the military at a time when funds were urgently needed for housing, industry, agriculture, education, and welfare. There was a similar situation in Egypt, Syria, Iraq, and Jordan. All the countries directly involved in the Arab-Israeli struggle encouraged a nationalism that impoverished their cultural and intellectual life behind a curtain of censorship. Other forms of intolerant fanaticism were encouraged, notably Jewish and Muslim religious extremism. Neither force did much to enrich the sum total of human understanding.

The conflict had broader economic and political consequences. Among these were the divisions opened up in the Arab world over the way to handle the Palestinian question, the civil wars in Lebanon and Jordan, and the strain put on Egypt after its reconciliation with Israel. Nations farther afield suffered too.

The leader returns — PLO chairman Yasir Arafat enters the Gaza Strip after his 1993 accord with Israel. Only time will tell whether the celebrations were well founded.

The Cold War deepened as the United States and the Soviet Union were drawn onto opposite sides in the struggle. This obliged both countries to increase spending on armaments and military aid more than they would have wished and may, ultimately, have hastened the collapse of communism in Eastern Europe. In addition to this two British prime ministers, Anthony Eden and Edward Heath and, some argue, the American President George Bush, had their terms of office shortened partly as a result of the consequences of the Arab-Israeli conflict. The reverse suffered by Britain and France in 1956 hastened the collapse of their overseas empires.

The terrorist campaigns that began in the 1970s and the economic crisis following the oil embargo ensured that the misery of the conflict was felt around the globe. The United Nations, established in 1945 to guard the peace of the world, proved incapable of arranging a final peace and was often converted into a place for conflicting propaganda to be aired.

THE STRUGGLE FOR PEACE

Ultimately the Camp David Accords set the tone for future progress in the conflict between Arabs and Israelis. This agreement proved it was possible for

Israel to forge a lasting peace with a former enemy, even handing back conquered lands in return for recognition and secure frontiers.

The next significant move toward peace occurred ten years after Camp David. By the late 1980s the PLO was coming around to the view that it could never defeat Israel in an armed struggle. It was also being encouraged by the Soviet Union — then winding down the Cold War under the leadership of President Mikhail Gorbachev — to reach a negotiated settlement with Israel.

The turning point came at a meeting of the Palestine National Council in Algiers in November 1988. Arafat announced that an independent Palestine could coexist with an independent Israel, and he renounced violence as a means of achieving the Palestinians' aims. The Israeli parliament was dominated by the hard-line Likud Party and was in no mood to compromise, but the United States immediately began talks with Arafat's representatives. With the Soviet Union on the point of collapse, the United States was now free to use all its diplomatic and economic power to encourage peace.

A number of factors initially held back any rapid progress. One was the opposition of the Likud Party to

Looking to a brighter future? King Hussein of Jordan (right) and Prime Minister Yitzhak Rabin of Israel meet beside the Sea of Galilee after exchanging copies of their historic peace treaty, November 1994.

Young Jewish settlers play in the snow above the settlement of Abir Yaacov on the West Bank. Settlements such as this one continue to pose problems to those who negotiate for peace.

Israel and Jordan End 46 Year Conflict
Israel and Jordan yesterday ended their 46-year-old state of war and opened the way for a full peace treaty. King Hussein of Jordan and Israeli Prime Minister Yitzhak Rabin signed a declaration on the White House lawn which says; 'The state of belligerency between Jordan and Israel has been terminated.'

The Independent,
June 7, 1994

negotiations with the PLO, whom they dismissed as terrorists. Other problematic factors were the *intifada* and further Jewish settlements on the West Bank. The continued terrorist attacks on northern Israel (over a hundred raids between 1985 and 1991) played into the hands of hard-line Israelis, as did continued opposition to Israel from Syria and Jordan.

The return to power of Rabin's Labor Party and the 1991 Gulf War finally broke the deadlock. In 1990 the Iraqi forces of Saddam Hussein invaded Kuwait, threatening the oil supplies of the Persian Gulf. The action drew widespread condemnation from the West, supported by a surprising Arab coalition. Early in 1991 a United Nations force led by the United States went to war to free Kuwait. In an attempt to draw Israel into the conflict and divide Arab opinion, Saddam launched Scud missile attacks on Israel. Approximately four thousand Israeli homes were destroyed and one civilian killed, but the government did not respond with force. Its restraint won worldwide respect and prepared the way for further negotiation.

In 1993 the United States arranged an historic agreement between Arafat's PLO and Israel. The Gaza Strip and parts of the West Bank have been given limited Palestinian self-government for five years while the terms of a final settlement are worked out. In 1994 Jordan, too, came to terms with Israel. It seems only a matter of time before Lebanon and Syria also reach a settlement with Israel. After almost seventy years of violence, there now seems to be a chance that the Arab-Israeli conflict will finally draw to a close.

GLOSSARY

absolutist
Having total power.

anti-Semitism
Behavior and beliefs hostile to Jews.

Arab League
A loose cooperation of Arab states formed in 1945.

arms race
A race between two or more countries to build up stocks of weapons.

attrition
Gradual wearing down of opposition.

authoritarian
Demanding obedience to authority, as in a dictatorship.

coalition
A group working together.

Cold War
Bitter hostility which does not break out into fighting.

colony
An overseas territory held by another country.

communism
The political system based on socialism and an all-powerful state.

coup
The sudden and violent overthrow of a government.

Crusades
The attempt of the Christians of Western Europe to capture the Holy Land from the Muslims.

Diaspora
The dispersal of the Jewish people by the Romans.

disengagement
Withdrawal from fighting.

embargo
A ban on trade or a single product.

emigrant
A person who leaves his or her country to live elsewhere.

enclave
An isolated piece of territory.

European Community
The former name of the European Union.

fedayeen
An Arab commando group acting mainly against Israel.

fundamentalist
A person who believes in strict observance of his or her religion and literal interpretation of religious writings.

Gaza Strip
The narrow strip of land along the Mediterranean around the city of Gaza.

General Assembly
The assembly of the United Nations in which all member states have a voice.

Golan Heights
The hills dividing Syria from Israel.

Haganah
A Jewish defense force established in Palestine in the 1930s.

Hezbollah
A Muslim fundamentalist group.

Holocaust
The Nazi attempt to exterminate all Jews living in their regime.

Holy Land
Palestine, or, more specifically, the territory around Jerusalem and Bethlehem.

holy places
Jerusalem and the places in Palestine mentioned in the Koran and the Bible.

immigrant
A person who moves into a country to live there.

infidel
An unbeliever of a specific religion.

intifada
The Palestinian uprising against the Israelis.

League of Nations
The international organization set up in 1919 to help bring about world peace, understanding, and cooperation.

mandate
A territory governed by another on behalf of the international community.

martial law
Rule by the armed forces.

Marxist
One who follows the ideas of the nineteenth century German socialist Karl Marx.

PLO
The Palestine Liberation Organization, the principal mouthpiece of the Palestinian people since 1964.

propaganda
Information or rumor spread to help or harm one particular point of view.

refugee
A person who flees his or her homeland.

right-wing
Favoring capitalism and free markets.

Royal Commission
An official British enquiry.

secular
Nonreligious.

Security Council
The decision-making body of the United Nations.

superpower
A major world power, usually the United States and the Soviet Union from 1945 to 1990.

Third Reich
The Nazi regime.

Zionism
An international movement to create a Jewish homeland in Palestine.

TIMELINE

1897 — World Zionist Organization formed.

1909 — Jewish town of Tel Aviv founded in Palestine.

1914–18 — World War I is fought.

1915 — With British support, Arabs begin revolt against Turks.

1916 — Sykes-Picot Agreement to divide Middle East between Britain and France is signed.

1917 — Balfour declares British support for a Jewish homeland in Palestine.
 — British occupy Palestine.

1920–48 — British rule mandate of Palestine.

1920–21 — Arab-Jewish riots break out in Palestine.

1929 — Arab-Jewish riots occur in Palestine.

1933 — Nazis come to power in Germany.
 — Organized anti-Semitism begins.

1936–39 — Major Arab uprising in Palestine takes place.

1937 — Peel Commission recommends partition of Palestine.

1939 — Strict limits are placed on Jewish immigration into Palestine.
 — World War II is fought (to 1945).

1945 — Arab League is formed.

1947 — Britain asks United Nations to resolve Palestine question.
 — United Nations votes to partition Palestine.

1948 — British leave Palestine.
 — State of Israel is proclaimed.
 — First Arab-Israeli War is fought (to 1949)
 — Problem of Palestinian refugees begins.

1949 — Jordan and Egypt take over parts of Palestine not occupied by Israel.

1952 — Nasser comes to power in Egypt.

1955 — First Soviet military aid is given to Arabs.
 — NATO arms are sold to Israel.
 — First Palestinian raids into Israel from Egypt begin.

1956 — Suez Canal crisis takes place.
 — Second Arab-Israeli War is waged.

1957 — United States proclaims "Eisenhower Doctrine" of support for noncommunist states in Middle East.

1958 — Egypt and Syria join in United Arab Republic.

1961 — Syria secedes from United Arab Republic.

1964 — Palestine Liberation Organization is formed.

1967 — Third Arab-Israeli War is fought.
 — United Nations resolution calls for Israel to withdraw from occupied territory.

1969 — Yasir Arafat becomes chairman of PLO.

1970 — Anwar Sadat becomes president of Egypt.
 — Palestinians begin campaign of international terrorism.
 — Civil war starts in Jordan.
 — Expulsion of PLO from Jordan occurs.

1973 — Fourth Arab-Israeli War takes place.
— Oil is used as weapon by Arabs.

1974 — PLO is given responsibility as representative of all Palestinians.

1975-90 — Civil war is waged in Lebanon.

1976 — Syrian troops enter Lebanon.

1977 — President Sadat visits Jerusalem.

1978 — Camp David Accords signed in United States between Egypt and Israel.
— Israeli troops enter Lebanon.

1980-88 — Iran-Iraq War is fought.

1981 President Sadat of Egypt is assassinated.

1982 — Israel invades Lebanon.
— PLO is driven from Lebanon.
— Massacre of Palestinians in refugee camps in Lebanon takes place.

1987 — *Intifada* begins.

1988 — Yasir Arafat renounces violence.

1991 — Persian Gulf War is fought.

1993 — Agreement between PLO and Israel is reached.

1994 — Agreement between Jordan and Israel is reached.

FURTHER READING

Abohdaer, David J. *Youth in the Middle East: Voices of Despair.* Watts, 1990

Anderson, Dale. *Battles that Changed the Modern World*, "20 Events" series. Raintree Steck-Vaughn, 1994

Bratman, Fred. *War in the Persian Gulf.* Millbrook, 1991

Cipkowski, Peter. *Understanding the Crisis in the Persian Gulf.* Wiley, 1992

Claypool, Jane. *Saddam Hussein.* Rourke, 1993

Cush, Cathie. *Women Who Achieved Greatness*, "20 Events" series. Raintree Steck-Vaughn, 1995

Dudley, William and Tipp, Stacey, eds. *Iraq.* Greenhaven, 1991

Hills, Ken. *Arab-Israeli Wars.* Marshall Cavendish, 1991

——— *1940s*, "Take Ten Years" series. Raintree Steck-Vaughn, 1992

Lawless, Richard and Bleaney, C.H. *The First Day of the Six Day War.* Trafalgar Square, 1990

Lehman, Emil. *Israel: Idea and Reality.* United Synagogue of America Books

Patterson, Charles. *Hafez Al-Asad.* Simon & Schuster, 1991

Pimlott, John. *Middle East: A Background to the Conflict.* Watts, 1991

Reische, Diana. *Arafat and the Palestine Liberation Organization.* Watts, 1991

Rogoff, Mike. *Israel.* Raintree Steck-Vaughn, 1990

Rohr, Janelle and Anderson, Robert, eds. *Israel: Opposing Viewpoints.* Greenhaven, 1988

Sullivan, George. *Sadat: The Man Who Changed Mid-East History.* Walker and Co., 1981

INDEX

ACKNOWLEDGMENTS

The publishers are grateful to the following for
permission to reproduce photographs:

Cover photo (large): Range/Reuters/Bettmann
Cover photo (small): Reuters/Bettmann

Hulton Deutsch Collection: pages 20, 22, 32, 36, 37,
38, 40, 44, 45, 53; Hulton/Reuters: pages 6, 66, 71;
Imperial War Museum: page 35; Magnum Photos:
pages 31, 33, 42, 47, 48, 49, 62, 67, 70; Peter
Newark's Historical Pictures: page 26; Popperfoto:
pages 8, 12, 13, 17, 65, 72; Range/Bettmann: pages
16, 41; Range/Bettmann/UPI: pages 23, 25, 28, 29,
52, 56, 57, 68; Range/Reuters/Bettmann: pages 7,
50, 51, 55, 59, 60, 61; United Nations: pages 63, 64;
UPI/Bettmann: page 58.